AF499229

Books by Borut Lesjak

Self-Love Healing series
Breathwork Healing
The Healing Power of Self-Love
Self-Love Healing Quick Reference
The Soul Syntax

Love Yourself Through series
Love Yourself Through Fear
Love Yourself Through Anger
Love Yourself Through Sadness

Sen & Sanja series
Sen, Sanja, and the Cube of Runes
Sen, Sanja, and the Clock of Mirrors
Sen, Sanja, and the Coat of Dreams

Mother Earth series
The Snowflake
The Cloud
The Wind
The Sun
The Tree
The River
The Snowman

Ink by Star series
Orion
Cassiopeia
Andromeda
Cygnus
Lyra
Phoenix
Canis Major
Aries
Taurus
Gemini
Cancer
Leo
Virgo
Libra
Scorpius
Sagittarius
Capricornus
Aquarius
Pisces
Ophiuchus
Pegasus
Ursa Minor

BORUT LESJAK

SELF-LOVE HEALING

QUICK REFERENCE

STUDIO BLEST

SELF-LOVE HEALING QUICK REFERENCE
Five Grounding Tools For Your Daily Practice
By Borut Lesjak

SELF-LOVE HEALING series, book 3

www.borutlesjak.com

Published by Studio Blest, 2020

Cover image by Ksenija Konvalinka
Interior art by Darja Klančar
Edited by Sarah Berti

Contents

Preface

In March 2020 I had a profound vision.

I was distinctly called to create a simple, down-to-earth, and pragmatic spiritual toolbox to help us all deal with the prevalent fear characteristic of these times.

The meditative techniques and tools I'd been practicing and teaching for years were something I trusted with all my heart. I knew they could bring about a positive turn in anyone's life if only given a fair chance: a steady, dedicated focus and light-hearted work over a minimum of four weeks—one lunar cycle, indeed.

Inspired, I chose to call this healing method the *One Moon Present* formula. The formula consists of five softly powerful tools: *grounding, staying present, breathwork meditation, creative writing,* and *learning self-love.*

The central tool is *breathwork meditation*, which is based on ancient pranayama yoga and then formulated and further developed by my dear friend and teacher David Elliott and of course, by my own experience and intuition. There is no doubt in my mind that breathwork is the singular most effective tool we have at our disposal today as individuals and humanity if we honestly want to awaken to our true conscious potential and bring balance to the world.

The soft, inner core of my healing method is *self-love.* We can only ever address anything in our lives in a lasting and sustainable manner if we embrace the reality of our circumstance, whatever that may be, and offer ourselves unwavering support through our emotional upheavals and rollercoasters, confusions, denials, and resistances. I call this attitude *loving yourself through.*

In the first series of books, ***Love Yourself Through***, I've collected deeply personal anecdotes related to fear, anger, and sadness. They are memoirs, assortments of intimate, transparent, and emotional stories from my real life. My choice was to open up and talk about the subtly meaningful or downright poignant events that marked, and even scarred one vulnerable boy, molding and shaping him by individual circumstance, personal responses, and in tune with untold family and societal traditions we pass on from generation to generation.

The three books of the series have a subtle, albeit specific intention: to stir, shift, and move the emotions of the reader and allow their old, deeply buried and denied memories to surface or resurface even when there was no prior awareness of any similar experiences. Sometimes we are inextricably trapped in behavioral patterns and traumatic stories that we may have inherited from our family lineage and we don't even know it because we're so used to the constant scents of negativity, abuse, or suffering in our life.

Some of the chapters overlap and touch upon either two or all three of the thematic emotions, and I wanted to include such recounts in all the books where they were applicable, even at the risk of repetition. (The three books are also available as a boxset or omnibus, titled *Love Yourself Through Fear, Anger, Sadness.*)

The reader is then heartily invited to work with the tools of the *One Moon Present* formula to open up to those past experiences and emotions in order to release energetic blocks and restore the flow of their vitality and well-being. The two tools that one needs here, *breathwork meditation* and *creative writing*, are described thoroughly in the appendix of each book. On top of that, I recorded a short 14-minute thematic breathwork meditation to be included free with each book, ready for the reader/practitioner to exchange with daily to strengthen their spiritual work.

Each of the three books of the *Love Yourself Through* series can therefore be regarded as a completely stand-alone resource to address the emotional challenges and bring about healing in life.

Nevertheless, I decided to craft another series of books, ***Self-Love Healing***, that delve deeper into the theory behind the *One Moon Present* healing formula and tackle even more general questions about the definitive healing power of self-love, the essential nature of consciousness, and the ultimate fabric of our underlying reality.

Book one, *Breathwork Healing*, is a concise workbook that introduces the reader to the formula's foundational tool, *breathwork meditation*. Enough theory and practical examples are provided for anyone to safely embark on their healing journey with this book as a trusty companion. If you feel you only need a few words and a slight push to get going this book may well be the one for you to start with.

Book two, *The Healing Power of Self-Love*, is the complete manual for the committed practitioner to explore the matter further and offer the inquisitive mind elaborate clarifications about how it all really ties together. Each of the five *One Moon Present* tools is described in detail so as to leave no doubts about their inherent potential and synergetic workings. At the end of the book, a sampling of my life stories is also included, both as a demonstration of the *creative writing* tool put to practice and as inspiration for the reader to witness that it is possible to heal one's life, no matter the starting point and the weight of past burdens. The theory presented is also condensed into clear cheat sheets and a glossary of lesser-known terms is provided. This is the book for you if you feel my healing method and the energy supporting it resonate strongly with your heart and soul.

Book three, *Self-Love Healing Quick Reference*, is a compact, concentrated edition of book two, provided for the experienced practitioner of the *One Moon Present* formula who wants to keep the distilled descriptions of the five tools handy at all times to revisit, or for the pragmatic beginner who doesn't want to focus on the theory any more than necessary when embarking on their healing quest for the first time.

As a quick announcement, let me reveal that I've been working on book four, with the working title of *The Soul Syntax*. Following my deepest inner guidance and intuition, I intend to freshly revisit some of the most ancient, million-dollar questions. *Who are we? What is our purpose? What is the true nature of reality and consciousness?* To be able to address these we'll need to redefine some well-known, conventional collective viewpoints, re-program our basic wisdom and vision, and even invent or create a new cognitive syntax that is not rooted in the human mind but in the pure consciousness of the soul. Who knows, perhaps we can co-create a way out of our common vicious circle of undeserved suffering, abuse, and denial, and ascend to our true birthright and realize Heaven on Earth now.

In addition to the books, I prepared a series of breathwork meditation recordings as audiobooks, ***Breathwork Healing Meditations***. They are full-length 28-minute recordings.

I can't stress enough the importance of meditating and using the breathwork recordings. In many ways, they are the primary and most elementary tools to work with as much and as often as you wish: they are both real and pragmatic. I meditate daily and I wish everyone could find the benefit, joy, and fulfillment of that in their own lives. There are no shortcuts to healing, but there is a direct route: breathwork meditation!

Whenever you feel willing to make a lasting difference in your life and the world around you, check out the meditation recordings and pick the ones that call to you. My own life changed forever the day I tried and did my first breathwork. A new hope entered then, a light arriving in the darkest hour, never to leave me again. I can feel it right now as I type this.

Are you ready?

I know you are—because you are reading this.

Introduction

Welcome to the quick reference to the ONE MOON PRESENT healing formula!

In this booklet, I did my best to present everything you need for your first step on your path of healing in a concise yet clear manner. I want to help you feel and know the essence of healing within five minutes of reading, so you will at once want to try the practical work with my 7-minute breathwork meditation, which you can access freely at this link: **omp7.breathwork.fun**. From then on, you will know how to proceed!

The intent of this quick reference is to introduce the basic healing tools that I've been practicing with and teaching for nine years—tools which may change *your* life for the better as well. I write further about healing and this powerful formula in my book *The Healing Power of Self-Love* and in my series of books *Love Yourself Through* that follow. Check the end of this booklet or visit **borutlesjak.com** for more information.

For all of you who seek change, perhaps because you feel that you got stuck somewhere in your lives, I devised a complete set of five practical tools that I'm calling ONE MOON PRESENT. These simple tools, when applied in a dedicated and steady fashion, will bring about life-changing and lasting results.

Nine years ago, I hit rock bottom myself. From the black pits of despair I saw no light of hope anywhere. My life force was spent so utterly that I wasn't even seeking healing at all. But chance, intuition, or Spirit—however you call it—brought me to a healer, teacher, and author named David Elliott and to his method of healing which is based on *self-love*—something I didn't know much about back then.

Sheer curiosity drove me to immediately test the central tool of healing: an ancient pranayama breathwork meditation which carries the power of opening our doors to the subconscious, soul, and mind, and shining light on our resistance, confusion, and denial. The power is in fact, ours—*yours*, dear reader—and we only have to do the work to claim it. And when I did the breathwork, all my hopes were restored from a seemingly hopeless situation, the way the glowing light of a full moon appears from behind a heavy cloud. So I rolled up my sleeves and chose healing in my life!

I firmly believe there is but one single requirement for our healing to happen: that we sincerely and consciously choose it. We don't need a perfect understanding or long preparations. As soon as we unconditionally decide on healing, Spirit gets involved in the process and takes over in a way so subtle that we may not be aware of it at first. It watches over us and supports our every step—even when it seems we are going backwards instead of forwards. And when I say Spirit, I mean a higher power of all there is—Mother Nature, the Universe, God—but I also mean your soul, your higher self, and your essence, because to me there is no separation between the above and the below.

Why do we even need methods, tools, books, and teachers, if our choice alone is enough?

We really don't. But when that's hard for us to believe, there's nothing wrong with helping ourselves in any way that feels good. When I lead my healing sessions and programs, I'm careful to step out of the way and leave the participants to sense their own power of love and to create trust in themselves and their own capacity of healing—the capacity to *be* a healer.

I prefer to work with tools of a practical nature, which help us to release the control in the mind and to consciously move into the heart—the seat of our true essence, our soul.

The scope of this quick start guide is limited, but in my book *The Healing Power of Self-Love*, I thoroughly describe these tools I use daily and which constantly teach me and bring joy and fulfilment to my life. In that book, I provide you with some basic theory—for the inquisitive mind—even though we can work well without it. However, I trust many will find it interesting. In the last part of *The Healing Power of Self-Love*, I share a sampling of stories from my life as inspiration and examples of putting this formula into practice. See the back of this guide for more information about *The Healing Power of Self-Love* and the other healing tools I offer.

If you decide to start with the shorter version—which goes straight to the work and tells you just as much as you need to know to embark on the journey of healing with ONE MOON PRESENT formula—this quick start guide is for you!

Upon subscribing to my no-nonsense newsletter you will also receive gifts, including my *Breathwork Healing* e-book, a 7-minute breathwork meditation, and a set of beautifully designed cheat sheets, containing concise instructions for your daily practice of the five tools of ONE MOON PRESENT.

And that is all you need for your healing!

So, are you in for a test-drive and willing to take another twenty minutes to leaf through this guide and try your first breathwork? That alone might get you to feel Spirit moving through you and convince you to commit to a daily healing practice for the duration of one moon cycle. Will you choose healing?

The choice is yours!

One Moon Present

What is the ONE MOON PRESENT healing formula?

Simply put, it's a set of individual tools and methods of healing, combined in mutual agreement and synergy that in time lead to life-changing and lasting results.

After years of experience with practice and teaching of healing in various formats, I gathered and intuitively arranged five key elements which I wholeheartedly believe will invite an unimaginable change to your life when used with steady dedication.

The formula works if you do *your* work, in an attentive, sacred manner. And when I say "do," I mean that you choose to bring healing into your life and you *exchange* with this method daily, as much as you can.

Where attention goes, energy flows. As you focus your attention on the healing exercises and meditation, your daily life energy is not wasted on old, self-destructive patterns of behavior, but is redirected to the fullness of your experience of beauty, joy, and love instead. The ONE MOON PRESENT tools helps you focus on the flow of energy.

The formula follows the moon cycle. According to ancient shamans, the time of the new moon is most propitious for the dreaming of new visions and opening to new paths. I invite you to start your healing work cycle then. But even if you join in later, the moon will help you get in tune with its rhythm, so there is no cause for concern.

For the duration of one moon cycle, 28 days, you will commit to devoted practice of all five tools of the formula—but feel free to adapt your daily schedule according to your inner needs and external circumstances.

Your healing will reach its peak at the full moon when clarity and the light of awareness will inundate you, and you will sense the support of Mother Nature the most—even though She truly does support you equally at all times.

Your healing cycle will end as the moon wanes and you ground the lessons received. Then you will be ready for a fresh moon cycle—a new spiral of awakening awareness and learning self-love!

If you want to get the most out of the ONE MOON PRESENT formula, I honestly invite you to keep *exchanging* with it in your heart, from day one on. Take your time with it—and take the time for yourself, for your healing. How important is that to you? Only you know.

> The ONE MOON PRESENT formula works best if practiced daily.

The subsequent chapters delve deeper into each of the five tools of the formula. If you read *The Healing Power of Self-Love* or have attended any of my events you can quickly leaf through and allow your intuition to point out anything you might have missed before. If you are new to this I recommend a more involved approach. But if you get bored easily by theory and a heap of big words, just save the theory for later and jump straight to the exercises.

For every tool, I prepared a one-paragraph extract at the top of each chapter. Also, special "cheat sheets" are provided at the chapter's end, with all the instructions you need for doing the work. And doing the work is key here—it's what will make all the difference.

Don't just take my word for it: try it!

Good luck.

Cheat Sheet: One Moon Present

START

Tool #1 — Grounding
Tool #2 — Staying Present
Tool #3 — Breathwork Meditation
Tool #4 — Creative Writing
Tool #5 — Learning Self-Love

↓

Repeat daily for 28 days

↓

SELF-LOVE HEALING

Grounding

Abstract

Once a day, take a minute. Stand up and feel your body. Close your eyes and use your other senses. Smile. Feel your connection to Mother Earth. Let go of all control and be aware of the Flow of Oneness.

Grounding is the simplest and most elementary of all the tools of One Moon Present. It's also the most crucial at the beginning of your road to healing.

It works best without any prior experience or knowledge—when you give in to trust. I invite you to treat *grounding* as a sacred ancient ritual.

Every day, at a time you may schedule in advance, pause and remove yourself from the everyday's noise, phones, internet, and television. Take a minute for your healing. Focus within, specifically on your body and bodily feelings.

Stand up. How does that feel? What do you feel in your legs?

If you have an opportunity, step outside and walk a few paces on earth, soil, grass, or pavement. Even if you are on the sixtieth floor, that's not a problem. Mother Earth encompasses all of existence.

> Pause to engage all your senses.

Now gently close your eyes and allow yourself to experience the world through your other senses. What do you hear? Listen to all the sounds, pleasant or not. Remember, you are grounding to the reality of *what is*.

What do you smell? Freshly mowed grass, blossoming roses, earth after the rain? Or the odor of a diesel motor? It's alright. We are opening to the world. We can feel we love it.

Do you feel the soles of your feet? What do you feel on your skin? Is there wind? Sunshine? Do you feel slightly hot or mildly cold? It's all good! You are alive.

Maybe you can even taste something? Some eastern spiritual schools talk about a connection between our sense of taste and a shift in consciousness. For example, you may discover a faint metallic taste in your mouth as your attention flows to your spiritual and energetic side.

Now *connect* to Mother Earth! This is what grounding truly means. Feel Mother Nature, smell her, taste her, sense her, intuit her deepest and sweetest essence. Love her. Touch her heart. Be her heart!

> Connect to Mother Earth and let go completely.

If you'd like, you can now open your eyes and look around. You are here. Perhaps you can now see the world in a new, fresh way.

Relax completely and let go of everything. Trust. Life is good. Love is in the air.

Cheat Sheet: Grounding

START

#1 — Silence your phone (and mind)

#2 — Stand up and feel your body

#3 — Close your eyes and smile

#4 — Listen, smell, feel, taste

#5 — Connect to Mother Earth

#6 — Let go of all control

#7 — Be aware of the Flow of Oneness

GROUNDING

Staying present

Abstract

Pause and look around you. Draw a deep breath and feel it in your body. Take your time and listen to your heartbeat. Remember you have a choice. Ask yourself who you truly are. Feel alive. Feel happy and grateful to be alive. Intend to stay awake.

Repeat many times a day.

Stop.

Look around you. What do you see? What attracts your attention?

The shape of a flower reaching upwards, a pair of pink and orange lamps by the TV, a wooden pencil on your desk?

Focus on one object. Stay with it. There's no hurry. Go deeper and feel the essence of whatever you are observing. Connect to it. Love it.

Now close your eyes and draw a deep breath. Let go. Simply be.

Take the time to feel your body, your organs, your tissues, your blood, your breath. Notice your posture, and whether you are holding any part of your body in tension. Is your spine proud and alive? Notice your jaw.

Open your eyes. Slowly. Who are you, right now? This is your life and now you are aware of it!

In a single flash, remember your own flow through time in the grand scheme of things, from your birth to your dying day. Are you aware of your impermanence, but also of your eternal nature?

We could say that staying present is the practice of constantly re-awakening to who you truly are—in this particular now. Who are you? Keep asking the question without looking for a definitive answer. Awaken to your deepest sense of your identity.

> Awaken to your innermost choice.

Now, in your imagination, go out there and imagine yourself living fully—as if your vision were already happening.

Staying present is meditation. You can practice it many times daily. Together with other ONE MOON PRESENT tools, it will help you awaken, first today, and then again and again. Gradually, your awakenings to a higher, expanded consciousness will become something normal—but never a routine. Routines and autopilot behavior are the opposite of consciousness. You can use the staying present tool, on the spiritual level, to break out of your routines.

Nobody really knows how we reach enlightenment. But when Spirit moves through us, something opens up. We become larger, more all-encompassing. Awake. Present. Clear.

I believe in tiny, quantum enlightenments that we experience every day. They can be stimulated by meditation. In my experience, a regular practice of breathwork meditation is the best for training and nurturing awareness. In addition, tools and techniques like *staying present* can be used practically anywhere and anytime to boost our practice.

In addition to the basic method for awakening awareness described above, we can help ourselves throughout the day by two other simple exercises.

The first one is called *quantum breath*. I recommend you do it many times a day, every day. I have my phone alarm set to alert me when it's time for *quantum breath*.

Quantum breath is powerful in teaching us to stop and pause anything we might be caught doing without hesitation, and take a single precious minute for our healing. As soon as the alarm sounds, we flip a switch and let go of everything else. We close our eyes and focus inwards. (Except when we are driving a car or babysitting toddlers!)

Quantum breath is extremely simple. You can breathe through the mouth or the nose, as you wish. First, inhale a slow, deep breath for the count of four—the unit could be seconds, or not, it doesn't matter—and you can go faster or slower, again, as you decide. Second, hold the breath in for the same count of four. Third, gradually release the breath out, while counting to four the same way. And lastly, hold your breath out, again for the same count. You just did four stages of equal duration: inhalation, pause, exhalation, pause.

That was one quantum breath. Repeat it three more times: four in total. It will take you roughly a minute to complete the whole exercise.

Be patient with yourself as you learn. After you get some experience with it, you can embellish the inhaling phase by visualizing, imagining, or sensing how your soul, or Spirit, is entering your body. While you hold the breath within, you can feel "complete, fully present, truly You." During the exhalation, you can imagine releasing everything temporary and ephemeral from your body and connecting directly to the Source or to all there is. And when you hold your breath out in the last stage, you can be aware of "being One with All."

I learned *quantum breath* from a mysterious teacher and a prolific and diverse creator, James Mahu of WingMakers.

The second exercise is almost too plain to call it an exercise, but it's incredibly effective. I borrowed it from shaman and author Carlos Castaneda.

Simply put, you will do your best to stay as present as possible when executing your everyday tasks. As a way to gauge how present you are, every time you put on your shoes or socks, or remove them, make sure you do the left foot first and then the right. You will see how often you find yourself forgetting all about it and performing this mundane task routinely, as we normally do.

> Intend to remain awake.

The key lies in developing awareness. As soon as you get used to putting your left shoe first and it becomes a routine for you—then there is no sense in practicing it any longer. At that point you should change the rules. For example, switch from *left first* to *right first*. And by all means, feel free to modify and apply this exercise to anything in your daily life. With this technique, everything that you do routinely can be used as a training ground for your awareness.

Cheat Sheet: Staying Present

START

#1 — Pause and look around you

#2 — Take your time and feel inside

#3 — Remember you have a choice

#4 — Ask yourself who you are

#5 — Feel alive

#6 — Feel happy and grateful to be alive

#7 — Intend to stay awake

STAYING PRESENT

Cheat Sheet: Quantum Breath

START

#1 — Inhale slowly for the count of four

#2 — Hold your breath for the count of four

#3 — Exhale slowly for the count of four

#4 — Pause for the count of four

↓

Repeat four times in total

↓

QUANTUM BREATH

Breathwork meditation

Abstract

Meditate daily with any of the breathwork recordings of your choice. I recommend using the specifically designed 7-minute meditation *One Moon Present* which you can find at this link: **omp7.breathwork.fun**.

I firmly believe this tool is central to healing and key to everybody's well-being in life. Practicing this powerful, gentle, and active meditation daily restored my energy, my hope, and my trust in love.

After more than nine years of staying present and exchanging with the meditation, I can safely say that it saved my life and my soul. Yes, I know: a bold statement, but one that I can testify to and show up for.

Even if you don't feel confident about using the other four tools, breathwork meditation alone will lead you, gradually and steadily, through the hardest days into more consciousness and self-love—simply by practicing it.

How is breathwork meditation done?

Simply put, you lie down on your back and breathe consciously through the mouth in a two-stage pattern while listening to a guiding voice and relaxing music. Near the end you start to breathe normally again, relax, and recharge. Keep your attention focused on your body and feelings, and let your emotions flow freely when they arise.

Before we delve deeper into explaining the breathing technique itself, I'd like to share a few words about the quantity and quality of your practice.

> Meditate as much as you can, even when it gets gritty.

Meditate as much as you can, even when life gets gritty—or especially then. Regular practice packs special power, but I find it better not to obsess about doing it *every* day without exception. We are human beings living in a real world and anything can happen. Let's trust we will find the time and be grateful for each occasion we are able to meditate.

> Treat breathwork as sacred.

Treat each time you practice breathwork meditation as a sacred ritual. Let the quality of your meditation be the best you can give to yourself. Sense your exchange with the meditation, breath, and Spirit. Therein lies all the magic. It is what makes the meditation special.

Meditate in a space where you feel good and nobody will disturb you. Relax comfortably. Get a blanket ready in case you get cold—when the energy starts to move, that can happen against all odds. You can use an eye pillow to cover your eyes and help the mind calm down even more. As you lie down on your back, don't prop your head too much—make sure your air passages remain clear. And—don't be too serious. Smile before you start.

> Why so serious? Smile.

Just before you start with the active breathing, it's the time to set your intention, or *intent*. Setting your intent is as easy as choosing what you want to bring into your life or remove from it. Trust your intuition and dare to follow your deepest dream. Choose the next step on your life's path. Create it. Feel what is calling you the loudest. And if your own dream scares you and you sense resistance—good! We can use that as fuel for self-love.

> Set your intent and feel it already manifesting.

You will breathe actively, always through the mouth, in a two-stage pattern: two inhalations, one exhalation. The voice on the recording will lead you and kindly remind you to keep the rhythm every time you get distracted and forget it. With the first inhalation of the two, bring the energy from the depths of the universe into your lower belly, below your navel, around the sexual organs. Use the second inhalation to lift the energy through the heart into the upper chest, almost to your shoulders.

> Two breaths in. One breath out. Through the mouth.

As you keep breathing like that, your heart will steadily open to a gentle and loving feeling of safety. You will focus on your sensations and create trust. Above all, you will give yourself permission to open your heart. To make that easier, you can recall fond memories and love.

> Focus on your feelings.

If any kind of resistance appears, you can choose to keep breathing. Breathwork is like a training range where we learn to develop consciousness—which we can then use in our daily life whenever we bump into a similar kind of resistance. If we are able to remain aware of our breathing and follow the two-stage pattern during all of our resistance, we can stay clear and present even through the hardest times and hardest emotions. That's how important our work with breath and resistance is. Our only task is to awaken from the grip of resistance every time it comes.

> Awaken from the grip of resistance.

In time, exchanging with the breathwork meditation will teach you more about yourself and about self-love. Each meditation will offer you the chance for a tiny enlightenment, which will add on and accumulate in your awareness. Sooner or later, you will be surprised to discover unexpected changes in your life: in a fresh way, you will be able to accept certain things that used to bother you or tax you emotionally. You will step into your own power of love—which is when everything changes.

> Self-love is key to healing.

There will come a time when you will sense a pleasant vibration in your body and nervous system during the breathwork—a vibration reminiscent of electricity, a tingling sensation, shivers, or just a variation of the temperature. That's the energy of your soul, or Spirit, flowing through you! It brings about healing on all levels: physical, emotional, mental, and spiritual. You don't have to understand or know anything—it is best to just get out of the way and let something larger than you do its work. For sure, our soul is ever present in our body for as long as we are alive—there can be no other way—but we can perceive our soul directly as the vibration of self-love only when our mind gets quiet enough.

> Witness your soul flowing into your body.

The last part of the meditation is called the relaxation or resting—or even healing phase. The recording will remind you to switch the breathing pattern to a natural one: one inhale, one exhale—either through the nose or the mouth. You let go completely and abandon yourself to an unconditional trust in the process. Remain lying down and feeling everything that is going on, knowing it's all part of the meditation, so you don't attempt to change or fix anything. Become aware of the energy flow, connect to it, and recharge your batteries.

> Revert to natural breathing and recharge.

At the peak of your experience, when you vibrate fully in the power of self-love, you will feel that your pre-established intent is taking place. The desired change—the new step on your life's path—is unfolding. In fact, you realize that it has already manifested! You will know this without a shadow of doubt—or else something in you will resist it. In such a case, be grateful to your resistance, because it is teaching you something, and in this state of clarity you are most susceptible to new insights.

> Feel your intent has already manifested.

Finally, return to your body and ground again, so you can continue with your day. Feel gratitude and congratulate yourself for doing the work. If you received any visions or messages from your soul, write them down into your journal diligently—and that is already stepping into our next tool of *creative writing*.

Ground.

A dedicated exchange with the breathwork meditation will lead you to unimaginable states. Spirit will start to move through you routinely when you go about your ordinary day, and happy accidents will follow you. Your intuition will grow and you will have no trouble trusting it. And you will be able to experience the vibration of your soul more often, even outside of the meditation.

Before long, your life will be changed. A new kind of hope will well up from your soul, one that will never leave you again. Then, you will be truly alive.

Enjoy!

Cheat Sheet: Breathwork Meditation

START

#1 — Make sure nobody will disturb you

#2 — Lie down on your back and relax

#3 — Put on the meditation recording

#4 — Set the *intent* for the session

#5 — Do the active phase of the breathwork:

- focus on your body and feelings
- breathe through the mouth only
- two breaths in and one breath out
- breath 1 in the lower abdomen
- breath 2 in the upper chest
- exhale, and repeat

#6 — Switch to the passive, or healing, or resting phase:

- breathe naturally through the nose or the mouth
- one breath in and one breath out
- keep resting and recharging
- feel your desired intent being manifested

#7 — Return to your body and ground

#8 — Write down any insights or visions you had

BREATHWORK MEDITATION

Creative writing

Abstract

Every day, after completing your breathwork meditation, write down your experience. Describe your feelings, emotions, and thoughts. Mark any repeating patterns. If you receive an insight or vision, record it in your log. Make up your new story and write it down.

Creativity is what helps us exit vicious circles of patterns and programs, against all odds. As we employ our imagination and intuition, and offer it our time and trust, a miracle happens.

> Creativity is Spirit acting through us.

Creative writing helps us focus our healing and ground it. It is more than just scribbling down words and sentences. It all starts with profound clarity and conscious observing. Doing that—together with practicing the other components of the ONE MOON PRESENT formula—will help us see through the fog of our denial and resistance. It will undo the knots that hold in place the veil of our old programmed story.

Our task of creative writing will be two-fold: to track our current or pre-existing condition, and to navigate ahead. With the former we embrace our past and with the latter, our future. As we heal to our completeness, they meet in the present.

The first aspect of creative writing is called the *Captain's Log*. We are all captains of our fates and we navigate the storms of our lives, but we also sail smoothly, sometimes under moonlit skies.

After completing your breathwork meditation—or at any other time in the day—write down your experience. Describe generally how you feel and where you are at. Write in some detail about your body position and feelings, your emotions, and also some of your repeating thoughts.

Focus on the extraordinary: whatever calls upon you or signals you. You don't have to transcribe every insignificant little thing, just record that which offers itself to you on its own.

> Write honestly about who you are and were.

Even when you don't feel like writing, make a small effort and mark it down, at least symbolically: just write a tiny minus sign in the log if you are absolutely reluctant to translate into words. Even a brief entry like that can sometimes hold you above the surface of a troubled water during your hard times and be the current that carries you to safety. Your willingness accomplishes this—the support you lend to yourself—and that is an aspect of self-love.

You can also write about your thought processes, but keep it short. Perhaps it's best to set a time limit such as five minutes. You will probably notice how repetitious your thoughts can get. Sooner or later we become bored by them. Then, it's time to gently release our old story and create a new one.

The second aspect of creative writing is the *Vision Chart*. You can keep it in a separate journal, if you wish.

Jot down all your visions, dreams, revelations, and insights you get during meditations or at any other time. Don't be alarmed if Spirit wakes you up at 3am only to reveal yet another beautiful piece of the mosaic you are weaving. Make a conscious, joyful effort to write it down in your *Vision Chart*. Then again, if you are exhausted from your busy day and would like to appreciate a good night's sleep—that choice is also valid. Remember, you call the shots of self-love.

When you feel ready, you can make up and create a brand new, fresh story for your life, and write it down. Take your time with it. Be specific and detailed.

Envision the innermost desire of your soul. Where do you want to go? What is possibly preventing you from realizing that?

> Dare to dream your wildest dream.

Before you put away your *Vision Chart*, close your eyes and deeply feel how the wheels of fortune are spinning and your new reality is being created for you.

Instead of starting from scratch, you can take a story from your *Captain's Log* and rewrite it for your *Vision Chart*. That's not cheating. In fact, it's a powerful way of out-creating your old story by intending a new one. Doing that, you address the unwanted and hurtful elements of your life and replace them with the healthy, wholeheartedly desired ones.

You will see. Creative writing is pure magic! It will change your life and the way you look at yourself. Who knows, maybe you will start to realize that you've always been a healer and a writer.

Cheat Sheet: Creative Writing – Captain's Log

START

↓

#1 — Prepare sacred space and time

#2 — Invoke conscious clarity about your life

#3 — Create a new entry in your *captain's log*:

- write down *where you are at* generally
- describe your *body position* in some detail
- *track* your feelings, emotions, and thoughts
- transcribe your *stream of consciousness*
- detect and report any *repeating patterns*

#4 — Ground your feelings about yourself

THE BEFORE STORY

Cheat Sheet: Creative Writing – Vision Chart

START

#1 — Prepare sacred space and time

#2 — Sense the sparks of your creative magic

#3 — Write down your new insights and visions

#4 — Establish and inscribe your future intent:

- where do you want to go next?
- what is stopping you?
- how can you love yourself through the block?
- make up your new story, with specific details!

#5 — Feel the manifestation already taking place

THE AFTER STORY

Learning self-love

Abstract

Each day find and write down another new aspect of self-love. When your wounded inner child is hurting, embrace her or him. Feel that you are in both states at once: loving and being loved. Trust love.

What is self-love?

I believe there is no universal answer and the real question is "what is self-love to you?" Not only that—it's vital you *feel* the answer. *Your answer.*

If I had to use one general definition of self-love I'd say it is an unconditional embrace of your *wounded inner child.*

The wounded inner child is a part of us that is disconnected from our whole being. A past trauma or a rough experience we couldn't cope with caused our awareness to split. Healing is the process of reuniting our pieces, and self-love is the super-glue.

Whenever we encounter a situation in life that resembles our original trauma, the wounded inner child gets triggered. We get lost in the diminished awareness of the wounded inner child, which is like a snapshot of our past consciousness. The mystery and nature of awareness is such that as we focus on the old memory, we become someone else in the present. We project the trapped emotions and negative expectations onto our reality in the now. The wounded inner child may be emotional in any way: belligerent, withdrawn, angry, sad, overwhelmed, resentful, or scared, and in a sense, we become the wounded inner child in that moment.

In such instances, when we act as if we were someone else, our inner response to our outward reaction may be antagonistic, because we can't accept the negative of our inner polarity. We are not okay with who we are in that moment. We judge it. We don't love ourselves. We don't love our wounded inner child, who suddenly appears to us as a foreign entity within our being. We want to get rid of that strange, unwanted part, but it is still a part of ourselves. And that is the opposite of self-love.

Self-love entails unconditional acceptance of who you are, even when you feel negative in any way—and especially then. I feel this aspect of self-love as if embracing my wounded inner child when he is suffering.

> Self-love is a state of being when you love a troubling part of yourself and feel loved unconditionally.

Learning self-love is a purely practical exercise. I find many people have trouble realizing the difference between thinking about self-love and actually experiencing it; they are not the same.

In your everyday life, pay special attention to those times when you hurt within. If you stay present with it you will be able to unconditionally embrace your wounded inner child, even though that will feel hard. Jot down every such case in your journal, perhaps another document, titled *My Self-love.*

For example, when I feel terrible guilt for not spending enough quality time with my kids when I'm super busy, I pause and close my eyes and envision myself embracing my wounded inner child, embracing my inner hurt. I don't judge it. I accept myself as I am. I love myself through it.

When your day goes by without any suffering and you are grateful for that, you can still apply yourself to find at least one new aspect of your self-love—your own fresh definition of self-love.

For example, "I'm a good father even though I'm sometimes busy." Or, "I know I'm doing the best I can as a partner." Or, "Even when I'm exhausted from a hard day, I can still be kind."

You can find a new gesture or a new way of expressing your self-love in practice. This can be anything at all. Perhaps you need two hours to yourself and a lavender bath with candles. Perhaps you need to not eat the chocolate cake, or you *do* need to eat it, or maybe you need to back out of an engagement you made, forgive a family member, or kiss your reflection in the mirror with a mischievous grin. Perhaps your wounded inner child needs to go outside and climb a tree. The choice is yours alone. Nobody else can know that for you.

If you commit for one whole moon cycle to staying present and lending support to yourself and your wounded inner child, many things in your life may change for the better.

Do as much of your healing work as you can. Feel that you support your own choices, whatever they are. You've got your back, and you know you can count on that!

Remember, it is your wounded inner child who is suffering and waiting for your embrace, waiting for your support of a true, unconditional friendship between you. You are both waiting to be reunited by self-love. What can be your next step? What can you do to help your wounded inner child feel safer and willing to come closer, to come back to you all the way?

Healing comes to us when we are patient and willing to be at our worst and our best simultaneously.

Find—no—*create* a way to unconditionally love your day, your life, and your self, and it will all come together! You will learn to appreciate the endless mystery of awareness in action.

Cheat Sheet: Learning Self-Love

START

#1 — Feel what self-love is to you

#2 — Write it down in your log

#3 — Each day find another new aspect of self-love:

- in what way is your wounded inner child hurting
- how can you embrace your wounded inner child
- be in both states at once: loving and being loved

#4 — Commit to trusting love and doing the work

#5 — Appreciate the mystery of awareness

SELF-LOVE

An example of a day on my healing path

In the snapshot of my typical healing day below, I omitted the "real life" elements of my schedule. One reason for that was to keep it simple and readable, but more importantly, I want to stress that ONE MOON PRESENT formula applies to all walks of life and ways of living. I trust you to fit it into your own unique timetable.

From as far back as I can remember, I've been practicing the marvelous tools of healing that I learned from many masters along the way. I combined and further developed the original tools, both through experience, as well as according to my nature and vision as led by intuition. I invite you to be inspired by my example, yet I strongly suggest that you trust your own ability as a healer and start tweaking and adapting any of the tools to your own personal preferences and circumstances.

After all, how boring would the world be if we all followed the same formula? This ONE MOON PRESENT formula is meant merely as a starting point, a catalyst of sorts to get you going—but may you learn to fly on your own as soon as possible. Generate your own trust, love, and wisdom and you will never have to seek it elsewhere again.

Good luck!

One Moon Present **Healing Day Example**

7:21	wake up and remember that life is good and I'm walking the path of healing
	…
7:34	(do yoga, tai-chi, tensegrity or similar exercises)
7:47	step outside onto the dewy grass and *ground*
	…
8:14	remember to *stay present* when putting on shoes
	…
9:00	use alarm to remind me to do a *quantum breath*
	…
2:00	use alarm to remind me to do a *quantum breath*
	…
3:54	remember to *stay present* when putting on shoes
3:56	learn a new aspect of my *self-love*
	…
5:13	embrace my wounded inner child when I feel hurt or scared
	…
6:15	use alarm to remind me to do a *quantum breath*
	…
7:06	do the *breathwork meditation*
7:20	do *creative writing exercise*
	…
9:15	use alarm to remind me to do a *quantum breath*

Healing is a sacred adventure

Indeed, it can be!

I invite you to approach this healing work softly, simply, with the merry curiosity and innocent enthusiasm of a child—and yet combine that with your hard years of experience, the sweat, the toil, the tears, and the search for healing in your life. The former will provide us with drive and passion, the latter with sobriety and balance.

No matter if you are an experienced practitioner or an absolute beginner, I warmly suggest you pay full attention, and respect your time when working with the ONE MOON PRESENT formula in order to receive as much as you can from it. The exchange will flow between you and Spirit.

Let trust enter your heart when dealing with these new tools, and they will help you on your way. Use them as your own, accept them in your life—you will see, they will make a difference if you give them a fair chance. But also, give *yourself* a chance. Therein lies the enchantment of exchange.

> The enchantment of exchange is in your willingness to trust.

Ultimately, it's key you do the work. You won't access healing by using your mind and theory alone. Consciousness expands through a steady and dedicated practice. True learning of your self-love unfolds in your everyday life. Only then will your shifts be lasting. It is great if you can weave this healing practice into your ordinary day without demanding any kind of special circumstances for your healing.

What do you say if we summarize the entire One Moon Present formula quickly now, together?

Let's begin! I recommend that every day—for one moon cycle, whenever you start—you allocate a bit more time for yourself than you usually do. During that newly available time slot, you can do the *breathwork meditation* and right after do the *creative writing* and *learning self-love* tasks.

There is nothing more to say about the meditation—just play the recording, lie down and follow the guidance. When done, get up and jot down what you feel, what you *don't* want to feel, and what you *do* want to feel. If you find any of it difficult to do, pause to embrace your wounded inner child—then write about that experience too.

Grounding can be practiced each morning when you get up, but you can approach the timing differently if you would like. Ask your own intuition. Or you can test several ways and times and sense where the exchange feels better to you.

You can attempt to *stay present* all day long. Or set an alarm to perform *quantum breath*. Or both.

And when you are having a bad day or when something triggers your wounded inner child to suffer—remember that is your best opportunity for *learning self-love* in practice, as it comes up, going through all the denial and resistance, unconditionally. Just as much as you are able to. Be gentle with yourself.

That's it!

Here's an even shorter version: just practicing the 7-minute *One Moon Present* breathwork meditation daily for 28 days will start you up. *Just by doing that*, you already stand a chance of awakening your consciousness to the point when your energy flow opens up and shifts towards your well-being and healing.

Try it. Or better yet: do it.

These are the times when we all need healing the most. Well, perhaps that could be equally true in any other era, but *you* are alive today and your hard emotions and hard times are here and now.

My intuition and experience with healing work leave no doubt (even) in my mind: our path to a fulfilled, meaningful and loving life evolves from a strictly mind-based state to an all-encompassing heart-based state of being—for the individual as well as for humanity.

The road is paved with our awakened awareness, the vehicle to move us on this path is self-love, and the fuel is our daily exchange with the whole of our reality: the good, the bad, and the yet unknown.

You are the one who can make a difference.

The choice is yours.

♡

Curious to know more about the five ONE MOON PRESENT healing tools? Get *The Healing Power of Self-Love* in your bookstore now at **hpsl.studioblest.com** and use the momentum to dive deeper! (FREE 14-minute meditation included.)

Author's note

Thank you for reading my book, *Breathwork Healing: A Beginner's Guide.*

In March 2020, I felt a powerful nudge as if Spirit had beckoned me, to show up and offer some direct and practical healing tools for everybody who was feeling the tremendous pressure under the harsh circumstances that had befallen us all. My first impulse was to write a book about fear and include a set of real stories from my personal life in it, alongside a description of the healing tools and the theory behind them. However, I realized that both anger and sadness should be equally recognized and touched upon, just like fear. So I set out to create a series of three books one after another. I call that series *Love Yourself Through.*

In the process of drafting the first book, I was distinctly guided to include five healing tools that work together in great synergy, and which I use daily in my own practice and teaching. Designing a cohesive, pragmatic healing formula, I chose to call it *One Moon Present.* The scope of this formula outgrew my original intention and I decided to publish it in a completely separate book, *The Healing Power of Self-Love.*

When the *The Healing Power of Self-Love* book was ready for release, I felt something was still missing: a brief, concise, quick start guide to the whole process of healing, the first stepping stone, so to speak. I did my best to produce this to-the-point booklet, *Breathwork Healing: A Beginner's Guide*, which in itself, I believe, is enough to open the avenue to anyone sincerely interested in healing.

Now you can be the judge of that in your own right and experience.

I remain humbled and grateful for your attention and for trusting my guidance. If the *breathwork meditation* practice indeed makes a difference in your life, and when you are ready for the next step on your personal healing journey, I'm confident you will find value and joy in reading the complete *The Healing Power of Self-Love* book. You can get it in your bookstore now.

All the best,
Borut Lesjak

P.S. If you like my book and want to help a wider audience find it and work with it too, please leave an honest review!

The Healing Power of Self-Love: About the book

Does negativity rule your life? Discover a transformational approach to reclaiming joy, peace, and love.

Stuck in an endless cycle of despair? Feeling blocked at every turn? Can't seem to find the light in your day? Experienced healer, teacher, and author Borut Lesjak has spent over twenty years helping clients overcome tough situations and find their way back to hope. Now he's here to share his straight-to-the-point suite of tools to heal those deep wounds in less than one month.

The Healing Power of Self-Love: A Spiritual Guidebook: Five Grounding Tools For Your Daily Practice is a thorough and well-organized handbook to restoration using the simplest of techniques. By following Lesjak's grounded daily plan and learning to stay in the moment with this highly practical approach, you'll soon feel the fog clearing. And as your own truth becomes clearer with each day, any anger, sadness, and hurt will evaporate in favor of a potent sense of feeling in charge of your own destiny.

In *The Healing Power of Self-Love*, you'll discover:

- A full, twenty-eight-day program designed to ground you in natural practices that rekindle your happiness
- An honest, direct, and caring manual to changing your life

- Powerful daily meditation and breathwork techniques to help you feel strong
- How to reconnect with simple, earthly emotions, so you're ready to take on any challenge
- Ways to embrace life no matter how it comes, energy healing tools, and much, much more!

The Healing Power of Self-Love is a pragmatic resource packed with no-nonsense methods to assist you in recovering your wellbeing. A companion to the in-depth *Love Yourself Through* series, if you like structured roadmaps and concrete tactics all wrapped in a loving methodology, then you'll adore Borut Lesjak's straight-from-the-heart toolbox.

Buy *The Healing Power of Self-Love* and begin your transformation today!

The Healing Power of Self-Love: A sample chapter

How do you feel about your emotions?

Emotions and feelings

There are three subjects I want to address specifically while talking about emotions: the distinction between emotions and feelings, states of being, and mood. These concepts are key to the healing method I use.

Let's start by pointing out the difference between our bodily feelings and emotions. For example, fear is an emotion, but the rush of adrenaline or a clamp in the pit of your stomach is a bodily feeling that accompanies the emotion.

When we face a difficult situation—especially in our tender age—our being may employ a coping mechanism called *denial* that protects our frail ego from being overwhelmed and possibly damaged. Emotions too harsh may be swept "under the rug," or in more technical terms, into the subconsciousness, to be processed and expressed at a later, more convenient time or in a safer space.

The problems occur when we keep suppressing our emotions for too long. We could say our emotions get stuck—and *we* get stuck with them. The balance and natural course of our choices, trajectories and lives get deranged, and we're not even aware of that. From our viewpoint, everything is just fine, until the body signals us a red alert by way of pain, sickness or chronic illness.

There is a powerful connection not only between physical feelings and emotions, but also thoughts. Every heavily repeating thought, or a thought form, or a belief you entertain, will be reflected in a corresponding emotion and a body sensation or a body posture.

> How do you feel about your emotions?

For example, if you routinely think of having to accomplish something to prove yourself worthy you might frequently feel the emotion of not being enough or of being empty within and you might even feel a fear of being alive. On the physical level, you may constantly slouch and feel a weight on your shoulders as if a heavy burden was actually present there, or you may feel "cold feet," or a certain emptiness or disconnection in your lower legs or ankles, almost as if your feet were not even touching the ground.

ONE MOON PRESENT formula takes all that into account and works with the interconnection of the mental, emotional, and physical levels, under the auspices of Spirit, the spiritual level.

In the example above, we may not be fully aware of our feelings of inadequacy or unworthiness, because they have perhaps been rendered subconscious. Consequently, we may live in denial of our exceeding ambition to succeed or of having to constantly compare and compete with others in order to soothe our wounded inner child and satisfy its need for recognition or praise. Many mind-created fears and problems may arise from such a condition.

The practice of ONE MOON PRESENT tools will help you become aware of where you are stuck, first on the physical level and then the emotional and mental mirror connections will become evident as well—when you are grounded and present enough and as the mind gradually releases its iron grip of control during regular breathwork meditations. Creative writing and self-love learning exercises will help you establish a new foundation for your balanced life, one full of joy and sweetness.

States of being

Some say that our emotions are located in the belly and thoughts in the head. I like to work with any coordinate system you might wish to use because we don't want to limit ourselves to the known and to what we're willing to believe. For argument's sake and for ease of explanation, let's follow the premise above.

So then, I ask you: what's in the heart?

If you say love, I agree. But what is love? Isn't love an emotion? Shouldn't it belong to the belly then?

No. You are right, because love is not an emotion. That's important. Love is a *state of being*. Just like peace and joy are. Again, we could use many coordinate systems and definitions, but deep inside, you know what I mean. There are levels of consciousness within that help us see love for what it truly is.

> Not all that you feel is a feeling.

A state of being is a consequence of awareness flowing through our being. The seat of awareness is in the heart. Our soul resides in our heart for as long as we're incarnated.

Now that's also the difference between true love (or unconditional love) and a conditional love which isn't even love at all. There are energies or aspects of energies acting upon us that we mistakenly perceive as love, but we're not going to talk about that here. For our work, it is enough to say that the feeling of butterflies in the belly isn't true love—and that's why infatuations come and go, especially when we're disappointed, hurt, or heart-broken—while true love is eternal and, yes, unconditional.

Another vital consequence of the distinction between states of being, like love, and emotions, is that while emotions are strongly mirrored in physical feelings and thoughts, love isn't and can independently co-exist with any or all emotions, feelings, and thoughts. Moreover, it mixes with them, it can embrace them and even transmute them to more love—not unlike fire and any material that can burn. Healing works because love is a state of being! We'll talk more about that in the next section.

During breathwork meditation, we patiently work with our energy and trust the breath to relax our mind so we can become more clearly aware of what is what—namely, of what love's true nature is: a manifestation of our soul dancing in our body. And while we open up to our stuck emotions and deal with our old hurts and physical discomforts, we still stay fully present with our love at all times. As we do that, we become aware of love and perceive it as a vibration which begins in the heart and then spreads throughout the body. We let it embrace all of our ailments, our imperfections and our problems, to make them go away—and love can really do that!

I firmly believe it is crucial for our self-healing method to work in a lasting and sustainable manner, that we do all our work ourselves, internally, by inviting the external agent—Spirit, Universe, God, Soul—to enter our sacred temple, the body. The responsibility and the power rest with us. It's all in our hands, and yet it isn't. It's a paradox that the mind is unable to unravel, and luckily, it never has to. It is enough to simply stay with the breath and remain conscious of everything we experience. Something larger than us—which is at the same time part of us—takes over and makes healing happen.

Mood

When I say mood, I'm not talking only about mood swings or moodiness. Simply put, mood is how we feel about our day, and also how we feel about our feelings, emotions, thoughts, ourselves, our lives and the world in general. It's a complex conglomerate of subtle, all-inclusive, omni-directional perception, both externally and internally oriented. It's where our feelings, emotions, and thoughts come together with our awareness.

For our healing process, it's vital we warm up to the idea that our mood is something that we may be able to choose, or intend—at least on some levels. It's not just an arbitrary emotional state that we get thrown into by circumstances. Mood is our response to the circumstances, and it is where our character shows—and depending on the clarity of our consciousness, we can avoid many pitfalls of prejudice, convictions, beliefs, and other programming, when we choose our responses to life's situations.

Another way of talking about mood is to liken it to weather. Of course, mood swings have been compared to weather before, nothing new here. The point I'm illustrating with this example is how the element of choice comes into the game—something we'll go deeper into in the next section. The feelings, emotions, and thoughts themselves may be more or less outside of our control, like most circumstances generally are. And our mood on a certain level may still not be something we can create or direct at will. But our perception of, and our response to our mood is already one level closer to the place of our command or choice.

> You are layered like a dream within a dream.

Back to weather. When it rains, we can't stop that. What we can do is make a choice: either we try to stay dry or we could choose to dance and sing in the rain. But even if we choose the former, we might still get wet involuntarily—it was obviously outside of our control. *Now* what we *can* choose is our response to what happened to us: we can get upset or just unhappy, or we can choose not to linger on it for long and instead change our clothes and get on with our day.

Going deeper, perhaps rainy weather makes us sad and such a response is beyond our choice—because of our subconscious programming. Or we may be trying hard to like the cold weather, but keep failing at it. And then we get disappointed by our failure to stay positive in that regard. So many levels there!

If we look at our feelings, emotions, and thoughts instead of the weather phenomena now, we may observe we have a similar response to them: our mood is our response. And then we have a response to our mood, which is mood again, but on another level. For example, if we get angry with our child for getting wet in the rain we may feel guilty because of our perhaps unwarranted or exaggerated anger. We may feel inadequate as a parent or even a failure as a human being, if we are inclined or programmed that way. In turn, our mood would probably shift to heavy and unpleasant. And if that is something that we experience often, we may have already anticipated it happening and feared it, or we may feel a leaden weight of being stuck in a vicious circle with seemingly no way out.

Thus, we've come a long way from an innocent accident of getting wet in the rain, through many levels of responses to a response (i.e. many levels of moods), and ultimately to a somber mood of "everything is wrong in the world" in a matter of seconds. The more we struggle to stay afloat, the more we sink into the quicksand of—trickery of the programming!

Before we discuss a way out of this nightmare, in the next section, one last definition. *Prevalent mood* is the general feeling about our life that we've settled upon: the way we see ourselves and our role in the world. For the example above, the prevalent mood could be depression. And the way we create and reinforce our prevalent mood to ourselves by the internal dialog we incessantly repeat in the mind, is what I call "our old story."

So how do we get out of there? The way out is through.

Summary

What did we learn in this section?

Feelings and emotions are not the same thing, even though they mirror each other, and they mirror thoughts as well. Love isn't an emotion but a state of being. It comes with awareness and coexists with emotions and uplifts them. Mood is our current, inner response to all of the above. There are countless levels of mood as we keep responding to our own responses. Prevalent mood is our overall response to ourselves and life in general. In the next section, we'll consider whether we are free to choose our prevalent mood unconditionally.

♡

Glossary

These definitions are merely guidelines or inspiration to help you open up to a new-story point of view. Some are included to clarify the more obscure or less common terms (e.g. *wounded inner child, pranayama, claircognizance*) and some are listed to expand the standard definitions of well-known terms, which are used in the *One Moon Present* book and formula in a new or different way (e.g. *mind, awareness, mood*).

abuse — Any expression or experience stemming from diminished *consciousness* and lack of *self-love* resulting in unbalanced *exchange.*

awakening — A temporary expansion of your *awareness.* Exercising awakening by daily *meditation* will grow your potential for a heightened *consciousness.*

awareness — Your essence and the essence of all there is: the stuff your soul is made of. Also, your knowing of the world around you and your attention to it.

belief — A mind-based *thought* form that focuses your energy to uphold your *old story.*

block — An interruption of the flow of your life energy, usually a consequence of a past trauma or inherited pattern of behavior. *Consciousness* softens and releases blocks.

breathwork — A central tool of the ONE MOON PRESENT formula. Daily practice of breathwork will help you nurture your *awareness* and *self-love.* The breath, when you *exchange* with it, carries the gentle yet unstoppable power of softening your emotional *blocks* and restoring your energy *flow.*

chi (or life force) — The energy flowing through your being for as long as you're alive. It can get obstructed or blocked. *Healing* restores its flow.

clairaudience — Intuitive hearing and speaking, based in the throat chakra, connected to the thyroid gland.

claircognizance — Intuitive knowing, based in the crown chakra, connected to the pineal gland.

clairsentience — Intuitive feeling, based in the heart chakra, connected to the thymus gland.

clairvoyance — Intuitive seeing, based in the third-eye chakra, connected to the eyes and the pituitary gland.

clarity — The opposite of *confusion.*

confusion — A mind-based perceived lack of sense, direction, and capacity for free-will choice. *Consciousness* clears confusion.

consciousness — A sublime, divine awareness of being aware, a state of being *awakened* or *enlightened*, a non-linear *presence* with all there is, externally and internally.

control (or the mind's control) — A tendency of the *mind* to protect your being by trying to direct absolutely everything.

creativity — A direct route to *healing* by transcending your *beliefs* and using *intuition* as the compass of your *soul* to guide your *free-will* choices and create your *new-story reality.*

denial — A natural mechanism for coping with an unbearable experience. May impede the process of *healing* when exaggerated. *Consciousness* exposes denial.

ego — An identification with anything less than the whole of who you are. Tightly coupled with the *mind*, the ego personality works tirelessly to protect itself—and you—against countless potentially harmful *beliefs*. May convince you to obsessively focus on fear, anger, or sadness and thus expend most of your daily energy for upholding your *old story* instead of creating healing in your life.

emotion — A movement of energy in your nervous system and your field of energy. Emotions can get stuck and may *block* your *flow* of *chi*, resulting in chronic fatigue, stress, discomfort or illness.

energy — The underlying source of all material existence, as opposed to *awareness*, the underlying source of energy, but also of non-physical existence.

enlightenment — Clarity and *presence* of awakened *consciousness.* The practice of ONE MOON PRESENT tools gives rise to frequent, tiny, quantum enlightenments.

exchange — Your *awareness* of the interconnecting *flow* of all there is. A sacred willingness to expand and open up to life, even in the midst of *resistance.* Giving and receiving freely of the essence of yourself, others, and the Universe. An unbalanced exchange *blocks* the *flow.*

feeling — A physical, bodily sensation, as opposed to an *emotion* based in your energy field and the nervous system. Feelings, emotions, and also thoughts are tightly coupled.

flow (or energy flow) — A natural state of all existence. When your flow is obstructed or *blocked* by stuck *emotions*, past traumas, or inherited *programs*, you experience a rift in *consciousness* where your *wounded inner child* gets disconnected from the whole, and you may need *healing.*

free will — Your soul-based capacity for making *choices* and creating *reality.* Can be obscured and confused by programming, patterns of behavior, and denial. *Consciousness* reveals and illuminates free will.

God — A common name for an unknowable source of all there is. *Spirit, Universe.*

gratitude — A direct route to *healing* by opening your heart, learning *self-love*, and balancing your *exchange* through appreciation.

grounding — A sacred ritual of pausing and connecting to *Mother Earth* and soul-based *reality.*

healing — A process of improving the quality of your life by learning who you are and how to love yourself.

humor — A direct route to *healing* by opening up to the *flow* and letting go of *control.*

inspiration — An avenue of soul-based communication that can be freely used against all odds, even through your worst mind-based *confusion*, *denial*, and *resistance. Breathwork* is an avenue to inspiration.

intent — An unknowable force of manifesting reality which you can't control but you can still use it in a mysterious way, especially during meditation.

intuition — A soul-based language of conscious *creativity*, as opposed to mind-based *thoughts.* A limitless, irreducible, and infallible expression of your *free will.* Your *soul* may intuitively communicate to and through you in many ways; also see *clairaudience, clairvoyance, clairsentience, claircognizance.*

love — A *state of being*, neither a *feeling/emotion* in the belly nor a *thought* in the head. Can co-exist with any feelings, emotions, and thoughts at the same time.

manifesting — Creating your reality by focusing your energy. It can be a *free-will* choice of opening up to and bringing in more *healing, love*, and universal *exchange* of Oneness, or a mind-based choice, upholding the diminished reality of your *old story.*

meditation — Any consistent and dedicated practice of *grounding* and relaxing the mind, and opening up to faith and your *soul* entering your body.

mind — A complex energetic organ of perception with the capacity of creating a virtual, mind-based reality, as opposed to a true, soul-based one. Neither negative nor positive, it can and usually is usurped and programmed by the stuck energies of past traumas to keep creating a mind-based *old story* of *suffering.*

mood — A current, inner response to your *feelings, emotions, thoughts*, and *state of being.* Also, a response to other responses in a layered fashion.

Mother Earth — A matrix for Humanity. A living, sentient being, unconditionally loving and supporting all living on Her.

negative — Anything we define by resisting it, fighting it, or running away from it.

new story — A story you create by choice to bring about a change in life.

old story — A story you repeat to yourself and which may keep you stuck in life.

pranayama — An ancient, yogic *meditation* technique based on conscious breathing, with countless variants.

presence — A conscious *clarity* about what is what, on the level of *awareness*, not thoughts.

prevalent mood — An overall response to yourself and life in general. A core building block of your *old (or new) story.*

quantum breath — A simple breathing exercise to train your *presence.* See the section on *staying present.*

reality — A relative and subjective manifestation that you maintain by focusing your attention. An interpretation of your internal and external perception. Either a mind-based construct, upholding your old story, or a soul-based conscious exchange with Spirit, opening your life to your purpose and fulfilment of your mission. Or an interplay of the two.

resistance — Any *feeling, emotion, thought*, or *mood* of *negativity*—or *positivity*—that may attempt to disrupt your process of *healing* by convincing you otherwise. *Consciousness* dispels resistance.

self-love — An unconditional embrace of your *wounded inner child.* A *state of being* when you love a troubling part of yourself and feel loved unconditionally.

soul — An inextricable aspect of *Spirit* pertaining to an individual being or many (potentially simultaneous) incarnations of a Being.

Spirit — An all-encompassing, eternal *awareness* and *consciousness* of all there is. *God, Universe.*

spiritual — An aspect of absolutely everything in life that is touched by the *reality* of *consciousness.*

state of being — A consequence of *awareness* flowing through our being, e.g. love, joy, peace. Sometimes confused with *feelings, emotions*, or *thoughts.*

suffering — A mind-based choice to diminish your experience against the free will of your soul.

thought — A unit of mind-based *energy* which can be focused in tune with your *free-will* choices or against them, thus accelerating or impeding your *healing* process.

vibration — A physical and energetic sensation of your *soul* or *Spirit* moving through your body and your being.

vicious circle — See *vicious circle. Healing* transmutes a vicious circle into a virtuous spiral.

wounded inner child — A part of you that is disconnected from your whole being as a consequence of a past trauma or a rough experience you couldn't cope with. When your wounded inner child gets triggered, your *consciousness* will shrink and your choices will be limited by *confusion, resistance*, and *denial.*

FREE Borut Lesjak starter healing kit

Subscribe to our newsletter at **borutlesjak.com** to keep in touch and be advised of the forthcoming sequels and other healing materials—get your **FREE Borut Lesjak's healing quick start kit**, including the **complete *Breathwork Healing* e-book**, the **7-minute *One Moon Present* breathwork meditation**, and the ***One Moon Present* formula's beautifully designed set of cheat sheets**. You will also receive invitations to **beta-reader copies** of my new books, and an occasional, never-before published chapter from both behind the scenes and from the great beyond.

If *The Healing Power of Self-Love* moved you a step forward on your path of healing, please take a moment to quickly rate the book or even write a brief review—ratings and reviews *truly* help grateful authors reach wider audiences and form growing communities of mutual trust—in love.

DO YOU WISH TO MEDITATE MORE?

Are you ready *and* willing to boost your daily spiritual practice?

The full-length, 28-minute meditation, *One Moon Present Breathwork Meditation* has been crafted under the auspices of Spirit and imbued with a clear intent of helping you honestly detect, lovingly address, and gently release any negativity in your life.

You can get the meditation at this link:

omp.breathwork.fun

Love Yourself Through series

If you seek healing in your life and are looking for a practical account from the trenches of somebody else's expansion that may inspire you to take your next steps, *Love Yourself Through* is one such report. Its formula continues where *One Moon Present* left off. Check out the series on **borutlesjak.com**, where an ever-growing compilation of transparent, personal stories are shared, working in conjunction with the five practical tools of ONE MOON PRESENT.

Love Yourself Through is a series of direct, hands-on workbooks with clearly defined tools, daily tasks, and goals. An ancient breathwork technique as well as other earth-grounded modalities are the integral ingredients to a conclusive formula called ONE MOON PRESENT that will transform your life within a single moon cycle. With a potent collection of inspirational stories as the main core of the *Love Yourself Through* books, and a practical, step-by-step guide, you will feel inspired and confident to address and recast blocked feelings or suppressed emotions, whether fear, anger or sadness. Revolutionize your life and experience well-being, health, joy, peace, and love every day—as a rule—not as an exception.

"Borut Lesjak is amazing and so are his gifts! He speaks his truth with pure love and first-hand experience, bringing to us the compassion and mission of a true healer striving to benefit humanity. He gets to the point and shares what works!"

—*Randi Maggid, vibrational shaman, breathwork healer & author*

You can get the three-book box set at this link:

lyt.studioblest.com

About the author

Borut Lesjak is an intuitive healer and author from Slovenia. Since childhood, he has been drawn to grok the mystery of existence. During the vulnerable years of his carefree youth, he awakened to the awareness of death and life, discovering a gift of claircognizance. Life hard-rocked the sensitive adult Lesjak to a state of hopeless haze until he ignited an inner choice to heal himself. Breathwork meditation coupled with creative expression opened his heart and mind to restore his innocence. Grounded by realness larger than life, he found his calling by bringing clarity, compassion, integration, and joy to this beloved planet for all to experience.

After residing and working in Australia, USA, Mexico, and Paris, France, he is now back in Slovenia growing roots with his wife and three children, offering healing work and writing books. He loves to dream, drive, travel, and hike. He is having fun.

You can connect with Borut at **borutlesjak.com** or stalk him on social media. He self-publishes, and personally reads and responds to his email at **borut@borutlesjak.com**.

"Borut Lesjak is a force of nature, and his unflinching, radical commitment to healing, growth and the transformative power of love is brought to life in *The Snowflake*, a gentle tale about the journey towards union and the magic of harmony with the wild world."

—Sarah Berti, mythmaker, author of the Helix Library Mythos

www.ingramcontent.com/pod-product-compliance
Ingram Content Group UK Ltd.
Pitfield, Milton Keynes, MK11 3LW, UK
UKHW021937190726
13853UKWH00004B/1511

9 798201 102975